Truly Foul & Cheesy™
Bayeux Tapestry
Facts & Jokes

Published in Great Britain in MMXIX by
Book House, an imprint of
The Salariya Book Company Ltd
25 Marlborough Place, Brighton BN1 1UB
www.salariya.com

ISBN: 978-1-912537-72-3

SALARIYA
SCRIBO BOOK HOUSE SCRIBBLERS

1 3 5 7 9 8 6 4 2

A CIP catalogue record for this book is available
from the British Library.

Printed and bound in China.
Printed on paper from sustainable sources.

Created and designed by
David Salariya.

Visit
www.salariya.com
for our online catalogue and
free fun stuff.

PAPER FROM

SUSTAINABLE
FORESTS

Author:
John Townsend worked as a
secondary school teacher before
becoming a full-time writer.
He specialises in illuminating and
humorous information books for
all ages.

Artist:
David Antram studied at
Eastbourne College of Art and then
worked in advertising for 15 years
before becoming a full-time artist.
He has illustrated many children's
non-fiction books.

Truly Foul & Cheesy™
Bayeux Tapestry Facts
& Jokes

This Truly Foul & Cheesy
book belongs to:

....

Written by
John Townsend

Illustrated by
David Antram

BOOK HOUSE
a SALARIYA imprint

Introduction

ATTAAAAACK!

Warning – reading this book might not make you **LOL** (laugh out loud) but it could make you **GOL** (groan out loud), feel sick out loud or **SEL** (scream even louder). If you are reading this in a library by a **SILENCE** sign… get ready to be thrown out!

Disclaimer: The author really hasn't made anything up in this book (apart from some daft limericks and jokes).

He checked out the foul facts as best he could and even double-checked the fouler bits to make sure – so please don't get too upset if you find out something different from a genuine witness to the Battle of Hastings, a sewing expert or anyone called Norman.

If I had my way, I'd RATify the lot!

Official

warning

With the Bayeux Tapestry returning to Britain (on loan from France), many people in the UK could glimpse this ancient stitched artwork for the first time. But please don't call it a tapestry as it's officially an embroidered linen cloth (a tapestry is technically woven thread, not stitched). As it's getting on for nearly 1000 years old (a bit like some of the jokes in this book), the famous embroidery may be a bit crumbly in places but not as cheesy as what you're about to read. Like those historical stitched pictures and words, the jokes here are well-worn, we're a-frayed (frayed, get it?). Things are about to get revolting in places so brace yourself for the grotty moth-eaten bits. You have been warned...

Loopy limericks

In this randomly foul cheesy mix
Of ingredients from ten-sixty-six,
Enjoy cheesy tastings
Of the Battle of Hastings
In a tapestry this book now unpicks...

On a tapestry strikingly old,
A story so priceless is told...
If it ever unravels
When it goes on its travels
The President's* blood will run cold
(Not the first time French heads
have rolled!)

*French President Macron

Riddles

First up – time to get some old riddles out of the way (after all, 1066 was the Riddle Ages!)

Spending a couple of knights in Hastings wasn't meant to be like this!

This is an ancient Anglo-Saxon riddle from before the Battle of Hastings. Who am I?

I was abandoned by my mother and father.

I wasn't yet breathing.

A kind woman covered me with clothes,

Kept me and looked after me,

Cuddled me as close as if I had been her own child.

Under that covering I grew and grew.

I was unkind to my adopted brothers and sisters.

This lovely woman fed me until I was big enough to set out on my own.

She had fewer of her own sons and daughters because she did so.

No wonder the Normans (from Normandy in France) decided to head over to Sussex in England and tell them far better French riddles like:

I'm a tiny rock that falls into a black sea. A silvery whirlpool and I disappear. What am I?

Hmm – not much better, eh? No wonder the English and French decided to battle it out. A quick reminder: when the Romans left Britain around 450 AD, England was taken over by Saxons from northern Europe, with a few Viking invaders from Norway adding to the mix. But Anglo-Saxon Britain changed forever in 1066 when the French Normans arrived.

Everyone wants a slice of Britain.

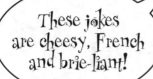

These jokes are cheesy, French and brie-liant!

Did you hear about the Norman invaders who tried to swim to England from France? They swam over halfway across the English Channel, but got so tired they had to swim back home for a rest. Doh!

Q: Who won this year's Conker Championships?

A: William the Conkeror

What started all the bother?

I thought a longbow was for tying big boot laces?

So, just what was the Battle of Hastings all about and what's the big deal? In fact, it was a VERY big deal because Britain was suddenly put 'under new management' and ruled by the French who had very different ideas. Quel dommage!*

Just a year before 1066, the king of England was Edward the Confessor. He was called that because he confessed his Christian faith and had the original Westminster Abbey built. His mother was French and the daughter of the Duke of Normandy. Edward lived for years in Normandy and, when he became King of England, many of his closest friends were Normans. He and his wife (Edith) didn't have children, so when he died aged 63 in 1065 there was a bit of a problem. Who would be the next English king?

*What a pity!

Now this is where things got messy. Edward apparently told his cousin Duke William of Normandy that he could come to England and take over the throne next. But on his deathbed, Edward also probably promised his wife's brother (Earl of Wessex, Harold Godwinson) that he could be the next king of England. Oh dear – both William and Harold were desperate for the top job.

Result = one almighty row.

Over my dead body.

I'm going to be king of England.

You need a good eye when it comes to arrows.

More fuss and bother

Harold was crowned King of England at the end of 1065, but within months others were after his crown (and his head with it). Just to make history even more confusing, another Harold wanted to be king. He was Harold Hardrada, the King of Norway, who turned up on the north coast of England with 300 ships packed with around 11,000 Vikings, to show he meant business. How annoying.

Fisticuffs

English King Harold was having none of this, so he and his Anglo-Saxon army rushed from London to York. Hardrada and most of his Viking soldiers were taken by surprise and killed in the Battle of Stamford Bridge. In the middle of King Harold's post-battle celebrations, who should turn up on England's south coast? Yes, William Duke of Normandy with all his French soldiers arrived in about 700 ships – upsetting the party.

We've come to invade Britain if that's OK?

Chaaargee!

It just wasn't one of King Harold's better Octobers. He'd only been king for a few months and now his French chum wanted him out. Harold rushed to Senlac Hill in Sussex to get a good view of the Norman soldiers gathering for a spot of bother. Even though it wasn't actually Hastings, this was the setting for a great big fight. On 14th October 1066, King Harold's troops and Duke William's troops (about 8,000 men on each side, although probably more French) clashed in a colossal battle for the future of Britain. It got very messy.

La Bataille d'Hastings

(A French yarn with a twist)

You'll have heard of the Battle of Hastings,
That happened in Ten-Sixty-Six,
When Duke William of France
Conquered England,
As a tapestry clearly depicts.

Chaaargee!

In the middle of chilly October
The Duke, in his warm woolly vest,
Hopped onto the Cross-Channel ferry
And sailed... sort of northerly-west.

Neither he nor his men had their passports,
Which was asking for trouble, no doubt,
As at Customs, the English were famous
For kicking all foreigners out.

As the Saxon King Harold gazed seawards,
To his troops on the cliffs, he gave orders:
'It's time for this country to signal to Europe,
And take back control of our borders.'

As the French rowed to England in convoy...
The sea was calm, gentle and still,
And after a full-English breakfast,
They arrived on the shores of Bexhill.

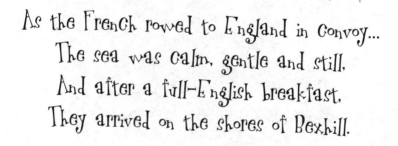

King Harold of England was waiting
In a deckchair right there on the beach,
Licking an ice cream and shouting
'Clear OFF!'
(A Saxon-type figure of speech.)

But William said, like a cool Frenchman,
'Sacre-bleu, I'll have none of your lip;
Get ready for battle, you Saxons....
We French are about to let rip.'

With one final lick of his cornet,
King Harold soon took up his stand,
With his soldiers all gathered around him,
And a dribbling ice-cream in his hand.

The Saxons kicked-off to advantage,
Brandishing spear, axe and sword –
But French Normans had stronger defenders...
When half-time came, neither had scored.

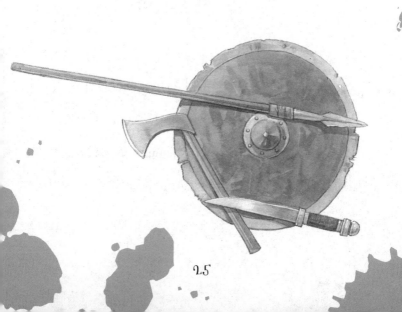

So, the Duke called his Normans together
And said – 'Get your arrows and bows
as we planned,
Then aim at King Harold in his deckchair,
With dribbling ice-cream in his hand.'

In a flurry of arrows and horses,
The Duke cried, 'I'll run down the pitch
And I'll score in a burst of French glory...'
But he fell in great pain from a stitch.

As he writhed in the mud, French Duke William
Let out such a gasp, then a cheer:
'King Harold has fallen but, what's more,
My STITCH has given me such an idea!'

As soon as the battle was over
King Harold slumped stately and grand,
In his deckchair, with an eye-full of arrow,
And a crumpled ice-cream in his hand.

Ahhhhhhhh!

The French were all set to take selfies
But William fetched needle and thread:
'We'll send home a dirty-great postcard
And weave a wall-hanging instead.'

With a swagger, great William the Conqueror,
In his crown, gold breastplate and breeches
Announced with a smirk that the Bayeux Croche
Would have everybody in stitches.

'I will show how the Normans were mighty,
While the Saxons played foul and uncouth...
Their defeat won't appear as a stitch-up,
But I'm bound to embroider the truth!'

Still today, like a long graphic novel,
The tapestry simply shows why
For the French... pride was won in the battle,
For the Brits... it was one in the eye.

Note – exactly 900 years later
England beat France in a rematch
at the 1966 World Cup!

Cheesy jokes

William, Duke of Normandy, insisted on bringing a boat load of French cheese with him, as he refused to eat English hard cheddar. But the Saxons attacked the French cheese boat and wrecked it. All that was left washed up on Hastings beach was a pile of de-brie.

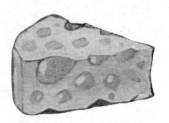

Rumour has it, the English taunted the Norman invaders with more cheesy jokes:

Q. What's the difference between Normans and toast?
A. You can make soldiers out of toast.

Q. What do you call 100,000 Normans with their hands up?
A. The army in surrender.

I'm not feline very well after that swim...

Q: Did you hear about the Saxon cat named one-two-three and the Norman cat named un-deux-trois? Both cats were swimming across the Channel for the Battle of Hastings. Which cat made it across and won?

A: One-two-three, because un-deux-trois cat sank (quatre, cinq)!

Q: What happened to the Norman archer who shot an arrow in the air?

A: He missed.

Foul fact

Before battle, the Normans tried to taunt the English by sending their jester towards them juggling his sword and telling cheesy jokes. His act didn't go well – the English killed him. Yes, the French jester was the first casualty at the Battle of Hastings.

Tough crowd!

33

Did you know?

The two armies at the Battle of Hastings fought all day, with thousands of casualties and hundreds hacked to death. William had the advantage of having more archers and horses. Bizarrely, mid-battle both sides took a break for lunch. Maybe Hastings Takeaways arrived! Eventually William's army won the battle when King Harold was killed. The earliest account of the Battle of Hastings told of Harold being killed and hacked to bits by four knights. (Unless the report said it took 4 nights to kill Harold!) The first report of Harold being shot in the eye with an arrow appeared years later. He was the last ever Anglo-Saxon King of England and his death marked the end of their rule... and the start of something very different (you'll find out more of that later).

King Harold was keeping an eye out for the French.

34

It was almost an arrow escape.

Fascinating fact
(for anyone called Edith)

The name Edith is a girl's name from Saxon times, meaning 'prosperous in war'. That didn't help King Harold, who had two wives called Edith (Ediths seemed to be everywhere in the Middle Ages). Harold had been married to Edith the Fair for about twenty years and they had six children. When he became king in early 1066, Harold married another Edith, the daughter of the Earl of Mercia. They had two sons (probably twins). Alas, Harold was killed at Hastings before they could know him.

Cheesiest joke ever...

On the day before the Battle of Hastings, King Harold said to his army commander, 'Are the troops ready?' 'They are, your Majesty,' said the commander, 'Would you like a demonstration of their firing power?' 'Yes, I would,' said the King.
The commander lined all the archers in a row and instructed them to fire. Hundreds of arrows flew through the air in a loud whoosh and landed a safe distance away. But one clumsy archer fired straight up and the arrow whizzed towards Harold – missing him by a whisker. 'You want to watch that fellow,' said the King. 'If he's not careful, he'll have somebody's eye out before you know it.'

Silly limerick

The prospects of victory were narrow
When King Harold got hit by an arrow.
All his soldiers retreated,
The English defeated...
And his body dragged off in a barrow.
(Result: Normans 1, Saxons 0, Hastings invaded by French tourists ever since.)

Hmm... why did we want to invade this place?

William the Conqueror

Just for the record

William became Duke of Normandy when he was 8 years old in 1035. Not everyone liked that idea and some French nobles tried to kill him. He grew up to be wary and quite a fighter. If someone upset him, he'd take ruthless revenge. In 1051, the people in a town William was attacking taunted him about his parents. That always made him huff and puff with rage. As soon as he was in charge of the town, he ordered everyone who'd upset him to have their hands and feet cut off. Yikes. Where there's a Will, there's a way!

William becomes king

Duke William became King William I of England two months after the Battle of Hastings. Saxon rebels kept popping up to show the French they weren't welcome, but William kept fighting to show he was the new boss. Once he took control of Dover, he battled on to take charge of Canterbury and Winchester before reaching London, where he was crowned on Christmas day.

I'd rather be at home for Christmas dinner.

Oops!

English nobles attending William's coronation cheered heartily to get on the right side of him. The trouble is, they were a bit too loud so William's soldiers outside Westminster Abbey thought it was an attack. They began to burn down nearby buildings in panic.

Just so you know...

Long after his death, King William became known as 'William the Conqueror'. His invasion of England, known as The Norman Conquest, meant that wine-drinking, French-speaking, castle-building rulers took charge of Britain for many years. And guess what? The name William began to spread in Britain and soon became very popular. Mr Shakespeare was very grateful.

A Cheesy teacher sketch

Teacher: Who did Duke William marry?

Pupil: His wife.

Teacher: She was called Matilda. Do you know when they married?

Pupil: On a Saturday?

Teacher: It was 1053.

Pupil: That's nearly five to eleven.

Teacher: They had nine children.

Pupil: That's enough for a football team if mum and dad played as well.

Teacher: Today's type of football wasn't played then. Do you know where William was crowned King of England?

Pupil: That's easy. On his head.

Teacher: It was Westminster Abbey – on Christmas Day 1066. Shortly afterwards he returned to Normandy.

Pupil: Maybe he'd left the turkey in the oven.

Teacher: Doh!

Pupil: So who made the big tapestry about William?

Teacher: Lots of people called Fred. That embroidery is made from hundreds of Freds.

Pupil: Doh!

Who really did make the Bayeux Tapestry?

(Maybe you're thinking SEW what?)

Shock…horror… the Bayeux Tapestry isn't technically French. It was made in Kent in England. It's only called the Bayeux Tapestry because it's been kept in Bayeux, France for centuries.

Did you know a mouse is on the tapestry? See page 78.

Question: What do you do if you win a great big battle, become king and take over the country?

Answer: You get your brother to post an amazing YouTube clip or put together a huge power-point presentation to show your achievements and tell your story. Or, if it's still the 11th century, you get him to organise an impressive fabric storyboard. In other words – the Bayeux Tapestry.

I have studied the tapestry and this is what I found.

Bishop Odo was probably the person who had the tapestry made. He was William's half-brother. Odo was Bishop of Bayeux in France. He fought in the Battle of Hastings, then became Earl of Kent. He appears in the Bayeux Tapestry as a key figure. Some historians think it was Odo who arranged to have the tapestry made about 10 years after his brother William became king.

Rude pictures? I'll have nun of it.

Silly joke

A nun working on the Bayeux Tapestry: 'I am putting in some rude bits to make people laugh. They'll be in stitches at my material.'
Another nun: 'You are a wicked sew and sew.'

47

10 tantalising tapestry truths

1 The pictures on the tapestry tell the story of events from 1064 to 1066, ending in the Battle of Hastings (but with the last part of William being crowned king missing).

2 This is the world's oldest 'comic-strip' at 70 metres long and 50 cm high. One guide says that, laid flat, it measures the length of three swimming pools (or maybe one big swimming pool!) Either way, whatever you do, don't get it wet or it will shrink and cease to be the longest embroidery in the world.

3 The arrow that supposedly hit King Harold in the eye was probably added to the tapestry in the 18th or 19th century during restoration work.

The tapestry shows 506 birds and animals (55 dogs & 202 horses), 41 ships, 49 trees, 37 buildings and 623 people. Only three of the people are women. One of them is Edith, the wife of Edward the Confessor. There is also a 'Mysterious Lady' and a fleeing woman.

Horses are the mane animals on the tapestry.

49

Apart from stitched pictures, there are sewn words in Latin – a language often used in documents of the Middle Ages (that's the medieval period of history in Europe from the 5th to the 15th centuries). There are 57 Latin captions in total across the tapestry.

There are just 8 different colours of wool in the tapestry: dark blue, dark green, light green, tan, blue-green, grey-blue, yellow and beige.

Think of all the sheep it took to make the tapestry.

During the Second World War, the tapestry was wrapped in sheets, sprinkled in moth powder and stored in a crate in a Paris basement, when France was invaded by the Nazis. Luckily it didn't get nibbled by rats.

8 Once the tapestry was finished, it was taken to France, but disappeared for hundreds of years. Eventually, it was found hanging in Bayeux Cathedral in the 18th century.

9 In 2013, the missing 'Finale' of the Bayeux Tapestry was re-created by over 400 people of Alderney in the Channel Islands. This was displayed in the museum alongside its historic original.

Why are you looking at me like that?

10 England made its own copy of the tapestry after a Victorian embroiderer called Elizabeth Wardle visited Bayeux in 1885. With a team of 35 embroiderers, the copy was completed and is still on display to this day in Reading Museum. The Victorian ladies added underwear to make some of the images decent!

I need silver thread and your whiskers are just right.

Talking of underwear...

You can get all kinds of Bayeux Tapestry souvenirs made from fabric printed with scenes from the Battle of Hastings: curtains, cushion covers, table cloths, t-shirts (even ones for teddy bears) – and probably stylish underpants as well.

Cue for a joke…

Did you hear about the visitor to the factory where the fabric is made? He fell into the loom making Bayeux Tapestry cushion covers. Doctors say he was badly bruised, but is now completely recovered.

At least he's now comfortable, fireproof and has lots of colour – so unlikely to dye.

Bayeux pun

The weavers of the Bayeux Tapestry had to work fast and under great pressure to finish on time. One of them got stuck when a technical error stopped her from entering her **PIN**. It was really needling her, so her boss told her to take a break and said, 'Just relax, you seam-stressed!'

Bad jokes annoy me, so I'm getting ratty.

Tapestry tweets

Harold's tapestry tweets

The first part of the Bayeux Tapestry show scenes leading up to the Battle of Hastings...

 Chat with King Ed about his French Cousin, William of Normandy. Might pop over for a free B&B. #cheapholiday (King Edward the Confessor talks to his brother-in-law Harold, Earl of Wessex in 1064.)

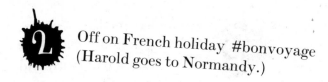

2 Off on French holiday #bonvoyage
(Harold goes to Normandy.)

3 I don't call this a warm welcome #yikes
(Harold is taken prisoner by the Normans.)

I didn't like my beard at first, but it's growing on me.

 Hmph – turned out to be a pony trekking holiday. #saddle-sore (Duke William of Normandy and Harold ride with soldiers to Rouen.)

 Now I've been roped into fighting their enemy next door. #getmeouttahere (William and Harold and the Norman soldiers become friends as they travel to fight Duke Conan of Brittany.)

 Yay – all good. Nice pressie from Will. #sorted (William honours Harold with a gift.)

 Promise to be best of friends. #greatchums (Harold swears an oath to William.)

Truly Foul & Cheesy Bayeux Tapestry Facts & Jokes

8 Back home for cosy chat with
King Ed. #jobmine
(Harold returns to England and talks
to King Edward the Confessor.)

9 King Ed pops clogs. #newkingwanted
(The death of King Edward the Confessor.)

10 Yay – I get top job. #partytime
(Harold is crowned King of
England on 6th January 1066.)

With all these
sick jokes, I'm looking
a little pail.

59

William the Tweeterer

Middle part: The Normans prepare to invade England.

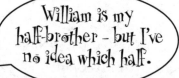

William is my half-brother – but I've no idea which half.

1 Not happy. I should be king of England. They promised. Odo agrees. #miffed
(Duke William, who believes he should be King of England, plans the Norman invasion with his half-brother Bishop Odo of Bayeux.)

60

Off to the docks to load ships.
Mustn't forget the garlic.
Still angry. #revenge
(Preparations are made for
the invasion fleet. Ships
are loaded with weapons,
armour, food, drink and
whatever else you need to
take over another country.)

We're off. Everything loaded including
kitchen sink. Nothing can stop us.
#feelingseasick
(The invasion fleet, led by Duke William,
crosses the Channel. Horses, weapons,
soldiers and pre-built wooden castles are
crammed on board ships.)

END PART:
The Battle of Hastings

1 Arriving in England. No one about. No duty-free shop. #boringseaside
(On 28th September 1066, the fleet lands at Pevensey, near Bexhill, in England.)

There's nothing like French baguettes when you're peckish.

2 Massive picnic near beach. Blooming seagulls. #birdpoo
(A feast is prepared, attended by Duke William and his nobles. Bishop Odo says grace.)

3 Unloaded flatpack delivery. Built castle. All ready. #whoneedsIKEA? (A portable Motte and Bailey castle is built at Hastings.)

4 Getting kitted-up. Horse in great shape. C'est formidable! #downwithHarold (On 14th October 1066, Duke William, in full armour, is about to mount his horse. The Norman cavalry rides off to fight the English.)

5 My troops are better than yours, so there. #goforit (King Harold gets ready to fight the Normans.)

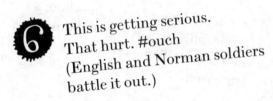

6 This is getting serious. That hurt. #ouch (English and Norman soldiers battle it out.)

7 Getting nasty. Bodies everywhere. #timeforlunch #kebabtakeaway
(The slaughter of soldiers and horses continues.)

8 I sock it to him. Eye socket to him – get it? #Harryhashadit
(The Normans kill King Harold, who is first shot with an arrow in his eye and then hacked to death by Norman soldiers.)

9 Got him. Game, set and match. England is mine. #yippee
(The Normans win victory over the English troops, who flee from the battlefield.)

10 Where is it? Last bit missing. #oops
(The coronation of King William in the Bayeux Tapestry has disappeared.)

Last Conversation between Harold and William (perhaps):

Harold: You eat weird food in France. Is it true you have frogs' legs?

William: Of course

Harold: Then hop it back to France and leave us alone.

William: How dare you. I will make sure one of our arrows has your name on it.

Harold: No worries – I'll keep an eye open for it.

SLURRPP

Tapestry tasters

Details in the tapestry have amazed historians for centuries. Try these...

1 Kebabs

Yes, believe it or not, the first recorded image of kebabs is on the Bayeux Tapestry.
Norman knights celebrate their victory over the Saxons by grilling skewers of meat over an open fire. It looks like whole chickens are cooked on spits, so maybe Hastings KFC were the caterers for the after-battle party. It looks as if the soldiers' shields double up as table-tops.

I think we've just invented the fast-food takeaway.

2 Halley's Comet

Time for a quick astronomy lesson. A comet is an icy body up in space that moves around the solar system. When it warms up nearer the Sun, a comet releases gases, sometimes showing a glowing tail. One of the most famous comets that can be seen from Earth about every 75 years is called Halley's Comet. Lo and behold, it showed up in 1066! Since then, the comet has appeared about 12 times.

The last time it was visible was in 1986, and it is expected to return in 2061. Most people only get to see it once in their lifetime if they're lucky. Maybe it was the last thing Harold saw with his good eye before another flying body struck. The caption, **ISTI MIRANT STELLA** means 'These men wonder at the star'.

William may have believed the appearance of the comet was a sign of good luck for him. It was shown on the tapestry in William's honour as a way to mark his success.

3 Another string to the bow

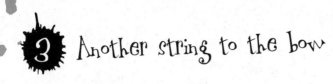

The Norman soldiers appear as the better archers, horsemen and fighters. That might be because the tapestry's story was being told from the winners' point of view!

Norman archers played an important part in the battle, especially after William ordered them to shoot high, firing their arrows onto the heads of the Saxons behind their wall of shields. Archers needed to move quickly, so they were lightly clothed and sometimes barefoot and bare-legged. Some are shown carrying their arrows in 'quivers' attached to their belts, while others take theirs from bigger quivers on the ground.

I'm all of a quiver.

JORKS

The Norman army would also have had skilled crossbowmen. Crossbows were a fairly new kind of weapon in 1066. They shot much more slowly than ordinary bows, but their bolts could smash right through shields and armour.

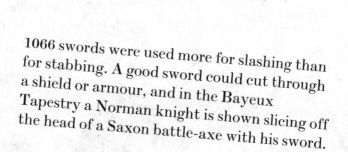

1066 swords were used more for slashing than for stabbing. A good sword could cut through a shield or armour, and in the Bayeux Tapestry a Norman knight is shown slicing off the head of a Saxon battle-axe with his sword.

4 A close shave

The figures in the tapestry have a lot of detail and you can tell the Normans and the English apart by the differences in their haircuts. The English have moustaches and hair to their shoulders. The Normans have neither beards nor moustaches and the hair is cut high at the back. At the time of the Conquest, the Normans were clean shaven and cut their hair very short, sometimes shaving the hair clean off right up the back of the head.

Another strand to the story

Apart from telling the main story of the Norman Conquest, the Bayeux tapestry is decorated around the edges with images from other stories going back hundreds of years. You may know some of the famous Aesop Fables that were supposedly told by a Greek storyteller called Aesop over 2,500 years ago. They were popular in 1066 and were added to the tapestry. As a fable is a story with a meaning, the ones included tend to say the same thing: it's not nice to be nasty and deceitful. Some historians think these may have been added by English embroiderers to get their own back at their mean Norman invaders.

If you've heard of the fable about the fox and the crow, you might know what's going on here.

The story goes like this...

A crow stole a piece of cheese, flew into a tree and perched with it in her beak. A fox was watching and wanted to get hold of the tasty cheese for himself. He needed to be extra sly and cunning. 'How beautiful you look today, you pretty crow,' he began. 'The beauty of your shape and the shine of your feathers are stunning. Oh, if only your voice could match your beauty. If you could sing as prettily as you look, you would be the Queen of Birds!'

The crow was flattered, but keen to show that her voice was, indeed, as good as her looks. She was determined to prove it so opened her beak to give a loud caw. The cheese dropped from her beak, and the fox sprang forward and gobbled it up. Licking his lips smugly, the fox looked up at the crow and said, 'My good Crow, your voice is right enough, but your wit and wisdom are lacking.'

Moral of the story: always be cautious of those who appear to be interested in you (like the French invaders who might seem to be friendly, but have their own selfish plans).

The fox and the crow appear three times in the tapestry, with the crow linked to King Harold and the fox to William. The cheese is a symbol of the throne of England. Harold has it and William wants it. William works out how to get it and Harold may have been as foolish as the flattered crow to travel to Normandy to be conned in the first place.

It's too gouda be true!

The wolf and the crane

You may know the next Aesop fable that appears in the tapestry...

A wolf had been feasting too greedily, and a bone was stuck in his throat. He couldn't shift it and could no longer swallow anything. That was bad news for a hungry, greedy wolf. He hurried over to the nest of a crane – a bird with a very long beak. He was sure that she, with her long neck and bill, would easily be able to reach the bone and pull it out.

'I will reward you very well,' said the wolf, 'if you pull that bone out for me.'

The crane was very uneasy about putting her head in a wolf's throat. That was high risk – and yet the thought of a reward was very tempting. After some thought, she did what the wolf asked her to do.

When the wolf felt that the bone was gone, he backed away and walked off.

'But what about my reward?' called out the crane.

'What?' snarled the wolf, 'Your reward is that you're still alive. Isn't it enough that I let you take your head out of my mouth without me snapping it off?'

Moral: expect no reward for serving the wicked. (Or, the message to English people after the Norman invasion might have been: expect no reward for doing what the French tell you to do!)

There's also the fable of the mouse and the frog in the tapestry.

By the way...

Aesop was well known for his animal stories and jokes – as well as his clever look at life. A story goes that one day, as he was enjoying a walk, he met a traveller, who greeted him and said:
'Kind man, can you tell me how soon I shall get to town?'
'Just go,' Aesop answered.
'I know I must go,' protested the traveller, 'but I want you to tell me how soon I shall get to town.'
'Just go,' Aesop repeated.
'This man is so rude,' the traveller thought and went on.
After he had gone some distance, Aesop shouted after him: 'You will get to town in two hours.'
The traveller turned around in astonishment.
'Why didn't you tell me that before?' he asked.
'How could I have told you that before?' answered Aesop. 'I didn't know how fast you could walk.'

He had a point!

A cheesy teacher sketch

Mrs A: I do like Aesop, don't you?

Mrs B: I've never tried it.

Mrs A: No, he told fables. They're in that French tapestry thing.

Mrs B: I don't know what you mean, dear.

Exactly, Mrs B.

This is utter twaddle.

Mrs A: You know – the Battle of Hastings. It inspired me to do a lot of French sewing.

Mrs B: Really? I did a bit of French sowing last week, too.

Mrs A: Crochet?

Mrs B: No, I sowed French beans, I sowed French marigolds and I sowed French garlic.

Mrs A: Doh! Here's a clue: Bayeux Tapestry.

Mrs B: No, I can't afford it.

Mrs A: Eh?

Mrs B: I can't afford to buy-a tapestry.

Mrs A: Doh!

What happened next?

So the battle was won, King William and the Normans took over the running of Britain and a large tapestry was made to tell the story. Was that the end? Not quite…

I'm the best ever Norman stone mason - and I've got concrete proof.

Soon after the Battle of Hastings, many English nobles ran away fast. Some left the country and fled to Ireland, Scotland and Scandinavian countries. By the time William the Conqueror died in 1087, England's Anglo-Saxon rulers had either escaped, been killed or were left as poor peasants.

The Normans spread through Britain, not stopping at the borders of England, but also invading Ireland, Scotland and Wales. Scottish kings were happy to let Norman castle-builders settle and keep building! In fact, the Normans have left us with plenty of their impressive buildings.

Did you know?

William reorganised the church in England. He brought men from France to be bishops and he built great cathedrals and huge monasteries. You can still see some of them – such as Windsor Castle, the Tower of London, Colchester Castle and Rochester Cathedral.

It's all so inSPIREing!

Good or bad?

Did the Normans make Britain better or worse, do you think? For some of the Anglo-Saxons it was good news, for others it was bad news...

Good news

Tax collecting can be so taxing.

1 The Normans brought in many new laws and French culture with them. King William organised the Domesday Book, which kept track of who owned what areas of land. That meant some had to pay more taxes.

William banned the slave trade and freed some of the Saxon slaves. By the end of his reign, their numbers had fallen and after another 100 years or so, slavery in England had practically disappeared.

 Norman-French and Anglo-Saxon words make up the English language we use today. For example, 'royal', 'law' and 'pork' come from Norman-French words, but 'king', 'rules' and 'pig' come from Saxon words. You probably didn't want to know that!

ᚢ᚜ᚺᛁᛦᛪᛁᚪᛁᛘᚺᚨᚱᛘᚺᛁᛦᚱᛁᛋᛁ

The French word for 'rat' is amazing - it's 'rat'.

Bad news

1 Although many people were killed in the battles of 1066, thousands more would die afterwards. In 1070, after English rebels and Danish invaders annoyed him, William attacked the north of England by destroying crops and livestock so that people starved. Possibly 100,000 people perished.

I'm not amooosed – it's udderly ridiculous.

The Normans treated women much worse than the Saxons had done.

 Tensions between the English and their new French rulers lasted for at least three centuries.

After nearly a thousand years, the English and French tend to get along much better. That's until they play each other at rugby!

For the record... England has won more rugby Grand Slams than the French. So there, William!

FOUL ALERT!

After 21 years as England's king, William the Conqueror met a foul end. In 1087, William was doing what he loved best – leading men into battle, sitting astride his horse in France. When his horse bucked, William was thrown forward onto a sticking-up bit of his saddle which 'ruptured his organs'. He died a few days later in agony at the age of 59.

As soon as he was dead, his attendants looted his belongings and left his body almost naked. That was a bit rude and disrespectful, eh?

Eventually, King William's rather large body was taken by boat for burial in Caen, but as he was being led through the town a fire broke out, leading to scenes of total chaos, utter panic and not much dignity for a royal funeral procession. The actual funeral ceremony in St Stephen's Abbey wasn't much better. It was interrupted by an irate heckler, who complained that the church had been built on his father's property without paying him. All very embarrassing in the middle of prayers for the king.

Even worse was to come...

So far you might think there hasn't been much that's really gross in this book. That's about to change. If you are easily disgusted, look away now…

As monks prepared William's corpse for final burial, they had to stuff his over-large body into a coffin that was a bit too narrow. As they rammed down the corpse with a great big push, William's bowels burst open with a revolting splodge, filling the abbey with such a stench that everyone rushed out holding their noses. What a smelly end for William the Pong-queror!

Limerick time

As King William was stuffed in his coffin,
A monk (a French scholar and boffin)
Said, 'Adieu, with our love,'
Then gave him a shove
In the box, which his innards blew off in.

Who next?

Just in case you wondered who came next after William the Conqueror as England's king, you won't be surprised to know it was his son. You'll never guess his name. Yes, William – he was known as King William II or William Rufus or William the Red because of his hair colour. He reigned for 13 years before he came to a nasty end in the year 1100, when his brother Henry took over.

William Rufus was killed by an arrow – which is a bit ironic seeing as it was said to be an arrow that got his father on the throne in the first place.

William Rufus died in mysterious circumstances while out hunting in the New Forest. He was found with an arrow in his back. No one knows if it was deliberate or an accident, but, because he was unpopular (to say the least), many people think he may have been murdered. Cue sinister music...

From William the Red to William the Dead.

Timeline - In a nutshell

1 January 4th 1066

The Death of Edward the Confessor.

2 January 6th 1066

Harold, Earl of Wessex is crowned King of England.

3 April 1066

Halley's Comet
appears.

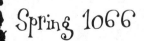

You won't
see it for another
75 years!

4 Spring 1066

Norman mission goes
to Rome to get the
Pope's support for the
Norman Invasion.

5 July 1066

William prepares his fleet for the English invasion.

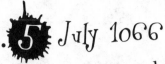

Once more onto the beach, dear friends...

6 21st September 1066

Harold marches his army to York to defend England against a Viking Invasion.

7 September 25th 1066

The Stamford Bridge Battle – Harold defeats 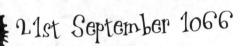 King Harald Hardrada and the Vikings at York.

8 September 27th 1066

Duke William sets sail for England – the Norman Invasion begins.

9 September 28th 1066

Duke William lands at Pevensey, on the South coast of England.

10 October 1st 1066

Harold celebrates his victory over the Vikings at York, but receives news of the Norman invasion. He marches his army to the south of England to fight.

Saturday 14th October 1066

The Normans and the Saxons begin the Battle of Hastings. A fence and a fosse (ditch) are built as Saxon defences. Each side taunts the other. The armies exchange blows and many Normans die in the fosse. The Battle rages for hours. Norman archers shoot arrows high in the air, striking the faces of the English soldiers. Many lose eyes as arrows fly thicker than rain. The English are unable to compete against French knights on horseback. The Saxon barricades are broken and soldiers march over heaps of bodies and crushed casualties. The wounded King Harold is killed, and his body mutilated by the Normans. English soldiers flee. William wins the Battle of Hastings – he becomes the Conqueror.

12 Late October 1066

The submission of the Saxons at Dover and Canterbury.

13 December 25th 1066

Duke William is crowned King of England in Westminster Abbey in London.

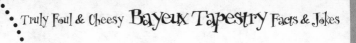

14 January 1067

William the Conqueror starts constructing castles in England: Norwich Castle, Wallingford Castle and Chepstow Castle.

15 Autumn 1067

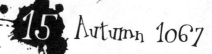

Odo, the Bishop of Bayeux, is made Earl of Kent and becomes William's Deputy in England.

16 Spring 1068

King William starts building Exeter Castle and the Tower of London.

17 May 11th 1068

King William's wife, Matilda, is crowned Queen of England.

18 1070

Rebellion against the Normans. Hereward the Wake leads the English with Harold's brother-in-law (Earl Morcar) against the Normans at Peterborough, but they are defeated.

19 1070s

The Norman Conquest is complete, and the Bayeux Tapestry is made in England.

20 1086

The Doomsday
Book is produced.

21 9th September 1087

William the Conqueror
dies near Rouen, France.

Time for
the king to be
THRONE away.

PHEEEEWEE

And finally (almost)...

How would you like to experience the Battle of Hastings for yourself? A re-enactment of the drama takes place each October near Hastings. For the 950th anniversary in 2016, over 1,000 soldiers in chainmail clashed swords, shot arrows and swung spears. There were no reports of major injuries and no one lost an eye.

English Heritage advertises the next battle like this: 'Re-live the atmosphere and tension, as over 600 soldiers clash in the infamous Battle of Hastings re-enactment. With a full festival atmosphere and activities to keep you awestruck, we're bringing the story of 1066 to life. Set foot in the Norman and Saxon encampments and learn about life in an 11th century army. Meet falconers and their majestic birds of prey, try your hand at archery and watch superb displays of cavalry horsemanship – perhaps even try a horn of mead.'

Tempted? You may just prefer the slightly more peaceful version in the warm and out of the rain. Yes, you've read the story, you've heard the jokes, now see the tapestry...

Tapestry on tour

For the first time ever, the whole of the original Bayeux Tapestry could be seen in the British Museum and maybe elsewhere in the UK after 2020. That sounds like a good excuse for some last dreadful jokes...

Apparently, the Bayeux Tapestry might go on display in the National Museum of Wales. When asked where in the building it would hang, the proud Welsh curator replied, 'We haven't decided yet. It will either be over by-there or right bayeux (by you).'

Did you hear about the woman who was rushed to hospital after the entire Bayeux Tapestry fell on her? Doctors say her life is hanging by a thread.

I don't think much of this wallpaper.

They should get something more modern to bring in the visitors.

'This magnificent Bayeux Tapestry,' said the old museum tour guide, 'is 944 years, 2 months and 14 days old.'

'Wow! Gee, buddy, that's so fascinating,' said an American tourist. 'How can you age that ancient artefact so accurately?'

'Simple,' answered the guide, 'it was 944 years old when I started working here two and a half months ago.'

Bayeux Tap rap

You wanna see a tapestry?
Then listen up as rappers see
A picture of the battle scene
With Will-i-am, yeah, that'll seem
Like he has won the victory
And conquers in embroidery!

King Harry was the wanderer
And Will-i-am the Conqueror.
Take a look at Bayeux, which is
In north France and full of stitches.
See that tapestry go touring,
Bringing crowds, how reassuring...
Yo, Will is crowned in majesty,
Go see the Bayeux Tapestry!

(Now try rapping that
in French – good luck!)

What a
twisted yarn
they wove

The threads of time, the twists and turns,
Reveal so many pictures...
The viewer sees the past and learns
From the labours of the stitchers.

Their handiwork still takes us back
To what they hoped we'd see.
Each stitch is just a tiny tack
In history's rich tapestry!

Q: What did the weavers of the Bayeux Tapestry say when they'd finally finished?
A: WEAVE done a brilliant job.

Q: What did William say when he saw himself in the completed Bayeux Tapestry?
A : Well, I'll be darned!

'Eye don't believe it!'
Yes, it's all part of life's rich tapestry.

'What you leave behind is
not what is engraved in stone
monuments, but what is woven
into the lives of others.'
Pericles (495-429 BC),
prominent Greek statesman

Good old
Pericles lived in the
Golden Age of Athens,
you know.

£10.66 – The Bottle of Hastings?

If you survived some of the truly foul facts and cheesy jokes in this book, take a look at the other wacky titles in this revolting series. They're all guaranteed to make you groan and squirm like never before. Share them with your friends AT YOUR OWN RISK!

QUIZ

1. Who was the English Saxon King in 1065?

a) Edward the Professor

b) Edward the Confessor

c) Edward the Successor

2. Who took over from him as king?

a) Harold Robinson

b) Harold Donaldson

c) Harold Godwinson

3. Who led the French army in 1066?

a) William Duke of Normandy

b) Norman Duke of Wilmandy

c) William Duke of Saxony

4. What killed King Harold according to later additions to the Bayeux Tapestry?

a) Boredom

b) A dodgy kebab

c) An arrow

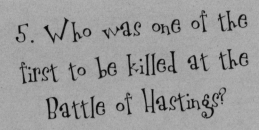

5. Who was one of the first to be killed at the Battle of Hastings?

a) An English cook

b) A French jester

c) A Scottish tourist

6. When in 1066 was William crowned King of England?

a) Christmas Day

b) Boxing Day

c) French Pancake Day

7. Which of these is shown on the Bayeux Tapestry?

a) A comet

b) A flying saucer

c) An elephant

8. Which of these appear on the Bayeux Tapestry?

a) Pictures from Bible stories

b) Faces of Roman gods

c) Animals from Aesop's fables

9. Which of these did William the Conqueror build in England?

a) Wembley Stadium

b) The Tower of London

c) Buckingham Palace

10. How did William the Conqueror die?

a) From a horse-riding injury

b) From exploding in his bed

c) From an arrow in his back

Answers:

1 = b
2 = c
3 = a
4 = c
5 = b
6 = a
7 = a
8 = c
9 = b
10 = a

GLOSSARY

Cavalry: troops that fight on horseback.

Earl: a rich British nobleman.

Hull: the framework, or main body, of a ship (including the bottom, sides and the deck).

Motte and Bailey: a type of castle with a motte (small hill) surrounded by a bailey (open area) inside an outer wall.

Normans: people from Normandy in France who conquered England in 1066.

Quiver: a case for carrying arrows, from the early French word 'quivre'.

Saxons: people who invaded England from Germany in the 5th century, who became the Anglo-Saxon people of England.

Vikings: people from Scandinavia who sailed to Britain and Europe and invaded from the late 700s to the 1000s AD.

INDEX

I finished reading this Truly
Foul & Cheesy book on:

........../........../..........